3-6

D1093294

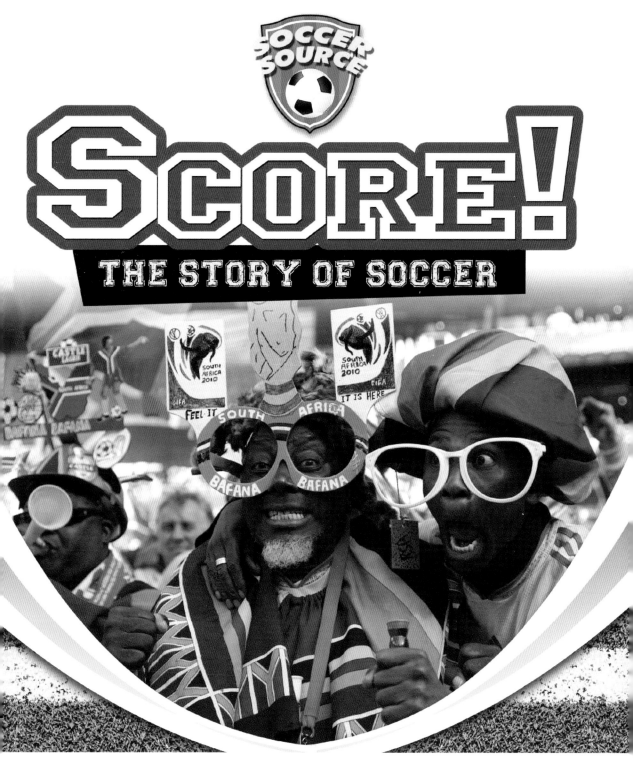

SCORE!

THE STORY OF SOCCER

Jennie Haw

CRABTREE
Publishing Company
www.crabtreebooks.com

Author
Jennie Haw

Publishing plan research and development
Kelly McNiven

Editors
Janice Dyer, Rachel Stuckey, Kelly McNiven

Proofreader and indexer
Natalie Hyde

Photo research
Melissa McClellan

Design
Tibor Choleva

Prepress technician
Margaret Amy Salter

Print and production coordinator
Margaret Amy Salter

Consultant
Sonja Cori Missio, International soccer correspondent, featured in The Guardian, Forza Italian Football, and Soccer Newsday

Photographs
Alamy: © Lordprice Collection (p 6)
Corbis: © Bettmann/CORBIS (p 23)
ZUMAPRESS.com/Keystone Press: © Tom Maddick (p 7); © DPA (p 12); © Koji Aoki (p 14-15); © Enrico Calderoni (p 15); © Imago (p 19); © Alan Schwartz (p 26); © Eduardo Maynard (p 29 top)
AP Photo: © ASSOCIATED PRESS (p 16);
Getty Images: Toronto Star via Getty Images (p 27)
Shutterstock.com: back cover; © fstockfoto (title page); © Travel Bug (p 4 left); © mooinblack (p 13, 21 top); © fstockfoto (p 17 bottom); © Martynova Anna (p 18); © photofriday (p 20-21 top); © jan kranendonk (p 20-21 bottom, 21 bottom); © Venus Angel (p 20 bottom); Photo Works (p 25); Iurii Osadchi (p 28–29 top); © Natursports (p 28–29 bottom); © CristinaMuraca (p 28 bottom), © salajean (p 29 bottom), © muzsy (p 30)
ThinkStock: © Dorling Kindersley RF (p 4 right)
Creative Commons License: © GFDL (p 5); © Reindertot (p 17 top)
Public Domain: p 3; p 8, p 9, p 10, p 11, p 14, p 22
Library of Congress: front cover

Created for Crabtree Publishing by BlueApple*Works*

Cover: An early 1900s photo of a U.S. soccer team
Title page: Bafana Bafana fans cheer before the start of the 2010 World Cup game between South Africa and Mexico.

Library and Archives Canada Cataloguing in Publication

Haw, Jennie, author
    Score! : the story of soccer / Jennie Haw.

(Soccer source)
Includes index.
Issued in print and electronic formats.
ISBN 978-0-7787-0242-9 (bound).--ISBN 978-0-7787-0251-1 (pbk.).--ISBN 978-1-4271-9432-9 (pdf).--ISBN 978-1-4271-9428-2 (html)

    1. Soccer--History--Juvenile literature. I. Title.

GV942.5.H39 2013   j796.33409   C2013-905784-6
                                              C2013-905785-4

Library of Congress Cataloging-in-Publication Data

Haw, Jennie.
    Score! : the story of soccer / Jennie Haw.
       pages cm. -- (Soccer source)
    Includes index.
    ISBN 978-0-7787-0242-9 (reinforced library binding : alk. paper) -- ISBN 978-0-7787-0251-1 (pbk. : alk. paper) -- ISBN 978-1-4271-9432-9 (electronic pdf : alk. paper) -- ISBN 978-1-4271-9428-2 (electronic html : alk. paper)
    1. Soccer--History--Juvenile literature. I. Title.

GV943.25.H396 2014
796.334--dc23
                                              2013033224

Crabtree Publishing Company
www.crabtreebooks.com   1-800-387-7650

Printed in Canada/092013/BF20130815

Published in Canada
Crabtree Publishing
616 Welland Ave.
St. Catharines, Ontario
L2M 5V6

Published in the United States
Crabtree Publishing
PMB 59051
350 Fifth Avenue, 59th Floor
New York, New York 10118

Published in the United Kingdom
Crabtree Publishing
Maritime House
Basin Road North, Hove
BN41 1WR

Published in Australia
Crabtree Publishing
3 Charles Street
Coburg North
VIC 3058

CONTENTS

Soccer has a very long and global history. One of the earliest soccer-like games was played in early China (255–206 BCE). "Tsu-chu," also called "cuju," was played with a leather ball filled with feathers and hair. To score, players kicked the ball through a hole in a cloth stretched between two poles.

Aztec Soccer

The Aztecs (1200–1500 CE) played a game that combined soccer and basketball called "tlachtli." To play, two teams moved a ball across the field without using their hands, or letting the ball touch the ground.

To score in tlachtli, players tried to pass the ball through a stone ring on the opposing team's side. The first team to score was the winner.

Ancient Greek and Roman Soccer

The Ancient Greeks and Romans also played a soccer-like game. The Greeks called it "episkyros," or "game," and the Romans called it "harpastum," or "ball." In both games, players kicked a small ball across a field, trying to get the ball across the opposing team's **boundary lines** to score. The teams were much bigger than they are today, with 27 players on each team.

Kemari is an ancient kind of soccer that is still played today at festivals in Japan. Players pass the ball to each other and try to keep it in the air as long as possible.

Training Regime

Ancient Chinese soliders played tsu-chu as part of their training. The Ancient Greek and Roman soldiers also developed their **agility** and speed by playing their own version of soccer. Although these games provided exercise and training for soldiers, they were also a form of entertainment. Many people liked to watch the games and cheer on the different teams.

SOCCER IN THE MIDDLE AGES

Soccer was very popular during the Middle Ages (500–1500 CE), particularly in England. Often called "mob football," games were **chaotic**, with no formal rules, no restrictions about who could play, and no limit to the number of players on the field.

Early Hooligans

These early games were very violent because players could do anything—including punch, kick, and wrestle—to get the ball from another player. The games were usually played in the country, but sometimes they were played in towns. Excited fans and players caused a lot of property damage, which upset many people.

*Mob football was so violent that people living nearby would **barricade**, or block, their windows during matches.*

Too Much Football!

In 1349, King Edward III complained publicly about his soldiers spending too much time playing "football." By this time, soldiers did not need to be as quick on their feet—it was more important that they be good **marksmen** rather than fast foot soldiers. Playing kicking games was no longer considered important training for soldiers.

Some historians believe that Roman soldiers brought the game of "harpastum" to England and that the first match between the British and the Romans took place in 217 CE.

The Royal Shrovetide Football match occurs annually in the town of Ashbourne. It has been played since at least the twelfth century. The two teams that play are called the Up'Ards and the Down'Ards.

Soccer continued to grow in popularity, especially in England. By the 1500s, many students were playing games of football at school. A teacher named Richard Mulcaster was one of the first people to encourage the use of **referees** because of the game's violence.

British Football

By the 1800s, there were two different types of British football. In the "handling game," players pushed and tackled to get the ball. They could catch the ball with their hands and run with it. This game developed into rugby. In the "dribbling game," players couldn't tackle each other or touch the ball with their hands. This became today's game of soccer.

Early players followed many different rules of the game before the modern rules of soccer were created.

Association Football is Born

As football became more popular, teams from different schools and **clubs** needed rules to follow when competing. In 1863, Ebenezer Morley established the Football **Association** (FA), to govern and regulate football. The FA was made up of representatives from different schools across England. The members agreed on the first set of soccer rules in London in 1863.

The world's first football club was the Sheffield Football Club, founded in 1857 by two British army officers, Colonel Nathaniel Cresswick and Major William Priest.

Soccer vs. Football

In most of the world, soccer is called "football." Because North Americans play a version of rugby football known simply as football, association football is commonly known as "soccer" in the United States, Canada, and Australia. In many countries, a soccer field is also known as a **pitch**.

A CHANGING GAME

With the new rules in places, soccer became much safer for players. Most players were male, since football was played in all-boys schools and men-only club teams. However, the new rules made it easier for women to play, and many did.

The Popularity of Women's Football

In 1920, 53,000 fans watched a charity soccer match between the Dick, Kerr Ladies Football Club (FC) and St. Helen Ladies' teams in Liverpool. Afterward, the FA banned women from playing on their fields. Some people believe that the popularity of the women's game upset the men of the FA. The FA did not lift their ban until 1971.

*The Dick, Kerr Ladies FC was formed in 1917 during World War I by female workers at a **munitions** factory.*

Pro Ball Begins

Although club football games were very competitive, FA rules did not allow players to be paid to play. In 1882, the FA learned that Scottish players on the Blackburn Rovers team were being paid. The FA declared that the payment must stop. The Blackburn Rovers didn't want to lose players who couldn't afford to play without earning money. They threatened to leave the FA and start their own league if the FA did not change the rule. The FA decided to make the change and teams were now allowed to start paying players —and professional football was born!

Some workers were given time off on Saturdays to play or watch football.

The Blackburn Rovers pose in 1884 after winning the Football Association Challenge Cup, the oldest soccer association competition in the world.

SOCCER AROUND THE WORLD

In South America, football began as a sport played by wealthy individuals. However, by 1914, it had spread to poorer neighborhoods and boys began playing games in the streets. Today, many South American countries are known for their very talented soccer players.

The Beautiful Game

A new style of football emerged on the streets of Brazil. The smaller Brazilians are known for playing with greater speed, style, and skill than many European players. They use their chest to bring the ball to the ground and move the ball quickly with their feet. Many fans consider the Brazilian style to be the most beautiful kind of football to watch.

Pelé (middle) is regarded by many as the best player of all time. He was the all-time leading scorer of the Brazil national team.

Football Travels East

In the late 1800s, British **colonists** brought association football to countries in Asia. Football grew significantly in the mid-1900s in countries such as Korea, China, India, and Japan. South Korea's national team is considered to be one of the top Asian football teams. In 1948, the team played in its first Olympics. South Korea has also played in many World Cup tournaments and has qualified to play in the 2014 World Cup in Brazil.

Two association football teams from Japan and Thailand fight for the ball in front of a stadium full of fans.

FIFA AND THE WORLD CUP

In 1904, the **Fédération Internationale de Football Association (FIFA)** was formed. FIFA is a **federation** made up of six national soccer associations. FIFA organizes major international tournaments such as the World Cup.

Uruguay 1930

The first FIFA World Cup competition was held in Uruguay in 1930. The World Cup, like the Olympics, is held every four years. FIFA chose Uruguay as the host country because its team had won the gold medal in both the 1924 and 1928 Olympics.

Today, over one billion fans watch World Cup soccer on television.

At the Centenario stadium in Montevideo, Uruguay beat Argentina 4-2 on their home soil to win the first World Cup.

FIFA's Growth

Today, FIFA has 209 members—more members than the United Nations! Its headquarters are located in Zurich, Switzerland. The first FIFA Women's World Cup was held in 1991 in China. The United States women's team beat Norway 2–1 to win the tournament with 65,000 people filling the stands to watch the final match. The next Women's World Cup will be hosted by Canada in 2015.

The Jules Rimet Trophy was the first trophy given to the winning World Cup team. The trophy was a model of Nike, the Greek goddess of victory. In 1970, it was given to Brazil in a special ceremony to celebrate their third World Cup win.

The 2006 Men's World Cup took place in Germany.

SOCCER IN THE OLYMPICS

Soccer became an official Olympic sport at the 1908 Olympics in London, England. In the final game, England beat Denmark 2-0 to win the first Olympic gold medal in soccer. The win came as a surprise, as Denmark had won their semi-final match with France 17-1!

Making the Cut

While most countries must qualify their team to play at the Olympics, a spot is always saved for the host country's team. In 2016, Brazil will be hosting the next Olympics. They will be looking to win gold at home after a silver medal finish at the 2012 Games.

The English national team at the 1908 London Olympics.

Going for Gold

Women's soccer exploded onto the Olympic scene in 1996 in Atlanta. With a home field advantage, the U.S. women's team won the first ever women's Olympic gold medal in soccer in front of a stadium packed with fans. The U.S. women's team has gone on to win the gold three more times in the 2004, 2008, and 2012 Olympics. Fans across North America are excited to watch the next Olympics to see if the streak will last.

Background image; Stadium at the London Olympic Games in 2012.

Did You Know?

Hungary has won the most Olympic gold medals in men's soccer with three wins in 1952, 1964, and 1968. They also won the silver in 1972 and the bronze in 1960.

Mexico defeated Brazil 2-1 to win the men's gold medal at the 2012 London Olympics.

PARALYMPIC SOCCER

The Paralympic Games are an international sporting event for athletes with physical and mental **disabilities**. They are held every four years, shortly after the Olympics have ended. There are two kinds of paralympic soccer: seven-a-side and five-a-side.

Seven-a-side Soccer

Seven-a-side soccer was added to the Paralympic Games in 1984. It is played on a smaller field but follows the same rules as regular soccer with some changes. There is no offside rule and players can take **throw-ins** underhand or with one arm. Athletes who play seven-a-side soccer have muscular **impairments** resulting from **cerebral palsy**, strokes, or brain injuries.

At the 2012 Paralympic Games in seven-a-side soccer, Russia won gold, Ukraine won silver, and Iran won bronze.

Five-a-side Soccer

In five-a-side soccer, all players, except for the goalkeeper, must have a visual impairment. A guide behind each team's net yells directions to help players when they are trying to score a goal. A **rebound** wall keeps the ball on the field and there is no offside or throw-ins in the game. Five-a-side soccer started in Spain during the 1920s. The first international tournament was held in 1998 in Brazil and five-a-side soccer was featured for the first time as a paralympic sport in 2004 in Athens, Greece.

The ball used to play a five-a side game has a bell inside to help the players follow it.

FUTSAL AND BEACH SOCCER

The Birth of Futsal

The name "futsal" is a combination of two Spanish words: "futebol," meaning football, and "salon," meaning indoor. Futsal began in Uruguay in 1930. It began as a mini version of soccer to be played indoors by **youth**, but quickly became popular with everyone!

Futsal's Popularity

Futsal is played indoors on a field about the same size as a basketball court. The game quickly caught on throughout South America and the South American Futsal Confederation was formed in 1965. Today, FIFA organizes the Futsal World Cup. It has been won five times by Brazil and twice by Spain.

Futsal stadium

Did You Know?

Futsal is played with a smaller ball which does not bounce as much as a regular soccer ball.

Futsal ball

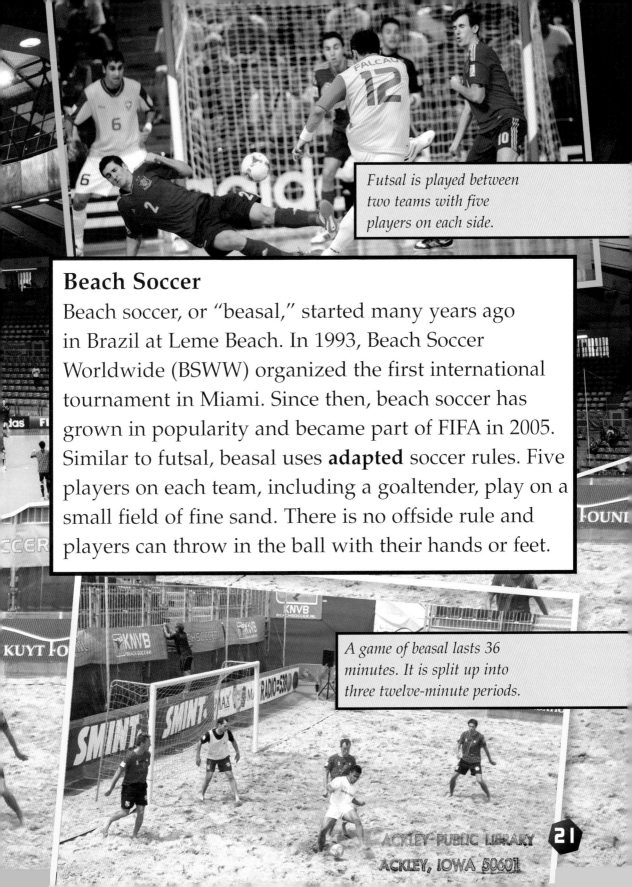

Futsal is played between two teams with five players on each side.

Beach Soccer

Beach soccer, or "beasal," started many years ago in Brazil at Leme Beach. In 1993, Beach Soccer Worldwide (BSWW) organized the first international tournament in Miami. Since then, beach soccer has grown in popularity and became part of FIFA in 2005. Similar to futsal, beasal uses **adapted** soccer rules. Five players on each team, including a goaltender, play on a small field of fine sand. There is no offside rule and players can throw in the ball with their hands or feet.

A game of beasal lasts 36 minutes. It is split up into three twelve-minute periods.

Soccer traveled across the ocean to North America in the late 1800s. British businessmen introduced football at Harvard and other colleges. Early leagues usually used the name "football" and games were played with 25 players on each side.

The Evolution of Soccer

However, at that time, college students were already playing rugby or an early form of American football. They were not interested in playing a "kicking game" using FA rules. The game then moved into working-class communities where interest quickly grew. By the early 1900s, many major American newspapers began calling the game "soccer."

The Fall River Rovers were one of the first soccer clubs in the United States.

"Canadian Rules"

The first football match between a British team, the Pilgrims, and a Canadian team, the Berlin Rangers, was held in 1904. The British players were surprised to learn that Canadian teams played by "Canadian Rules." These rules allowed players to be more physical, meaning players could trip each other. The Canadian team beat the British 2–1. The British team complained about their aggressive playing. However, by 1908, the "Canadian Rules" were replaced as Canadian teams began to follow traditional FA rules. Unlike the United States, in Canada it was not until after 1945 that football came to be commonly called soccer.

Early Canadian soccer players were know for playing rough during a game.

A GROWING POPULARITY

After World War I, many people from Britain moved to North America. This helped encourage the growth of soccer. However, during World War II, many players went overseas to fight and many football organizations in North America closed down. After the war, football had to be rebuilt.

American Soccer Associations

The United States Soccer Federation (USSF) has governed soccer across the country since 1913. The sport has struggled to compete with baseball, football, basketball, and hockey. In 2009, the United States formed the Women's Professional Soccer (WPS) league. It ended in 2012. The National Women's Soccer League (NWSL) began playing in spring 2013 with eight teams.

Canadian Soccer Associations

Since 1912, soccer in Canada has been governed by the Dominion of Canada Football Association. Its name was changed to the Canadian Soccer Association (CSA) in 1971. The first professional soccer league in Canada was formed in 1926 and was called the National Soccer League (NSL).

Major League Soccer

The MLS, or Major League Soccer, was formed in 1993. It currently has 16 American teams and three Canadian teams and is divided into two **conferences**, or groups.

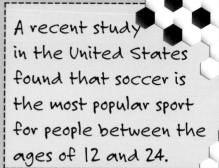

A recent study in the United States found that soccer is the most popular sport for people between the ages of 12 and 24.

Eastern Conference

Chicago Fire
Columbus Crew
D.C. United
Houston Dynamo
Montreal Impact
New England Revolution
New York Red Bulls
Philadelphia Union
Sporting Kansas City
Toronto FC

Western Conference

Chivas USA
Colorado Rapids
FC Dallas
Los Angeles Galaxy
Portland Timbers
Real Salt Lake
San Jose Earthquakes
Seattle Sounders FC
Vancouver Whitecaps FC

Clint Dempsey, (left) is the current captain of the U.S. men's national soccer team. He also plays for the Seattle Sounders in the MLS.

WOMEN AND SOCCER

Women have always played football, often with little recognition or encouragement. Times have changed. Today, young girls and women from many countries around the world are encouraged to play soccer and participate in competitions and professional leagues.

Leveling the Field

In the past, most schools in the United States only had soccer teams for boys. This changed in 1972 when a law was passed called Title IX. This new law required schools to provide equal opportunities for both boys and girls in sports. Schools that only had a boy's soccer team had to also develop a girl's team if they wanted to receive money for sports from the government.

As young athletes, superstars such as Abby Wambach, were given more opportunities to play, thanks to Title IX!

Healthy Competition

In recent years, women's soccer in North America has captured the imagination of many fans. Both the United States and Canada have strong women's teams that are fierce competitors on the international scene. At the 2012 London Olympics, the two teams met in the semi-finals. In a close match, the U.S. team beat the Canadians 4-3. The U.S. team moved on to win the gold medal and Canada captured the bronze. When these two teams play, fans always enjoy an exciting game!

The U.S. women's soccer team has won the Women's World Cup twice in 1991 and 1999.

Almost 22,500 fans watched a game between the U.S. and Canada at BMO field in Toronto in July 2013. The U.S. won again, much to the Canadian fans' disappointment.

FANS AND FAIR PLAY

Soccer fans are known around the world for their endless love of the game and enthusiastic spirit. The world record for the most fans at one soccer game was set in 1950, when 199,854 fans packed the stands to cheer at the 1950 World Cup final in Brazil.

Fans in a Frenzy

Sometimes, soccer fans have taken the game a little too seriously. In the 1960s, **hooliganism**, or violent behavior, became a growing problem at soccer matches, particularly in England. It is important to remember that as exciting a game as soccer is, good sportsmanship is important for players, officials, and also the fans in the stands.

Soccer riots are a large issue in some countries. Police are often called in to deal with soccer violence.

Soccer Mascots

International tournaments such as the FIFA World Cup have unique mascots to help get fans excited for upcoming tournaments. Each mascot represents something fun and unique about the host country.

Fuleco the armadillo is the mascot for the 2014 World Cup.

Did You Know?

Fuleco's name is a combination of the Spanish word for football, "futebol" and ecology, "ecologia."

Fair Play

In 1997, FIFA developed the Fair Play rules and program to promote the value of fair play in soccer among both players and fans.

One of the ten rules in this list is to "respect opponents, teammates, referees, officials, and spectators." This rule also means that fans should respect each other, players, referees, and officials as well.

Showing respect for the opposing team players and referees is a mark of true sportsmanship.

THE FUTURE IS BRIGHT

Soccer as a sport has come a long way from ancient kicking games to being one of the world's most loved and popular sports. The excitement continues as the sport is always changing. Tournaments and leagues are growing; talented, young superstars are taking to the field every day; and new technologies are changing how the game is played. Whether you watch soccer, play soccer, or both, it is fun to be a part of this exciting sport!

LEARNING MORE

Books

Gifford, Clive. *The Business of Soccer*. Rosen Publishing, 2011.

Hurley, Michael. *World of Soccer*. Capstone Press, 2010.

Kelley, K. C. *Soccer*. Cherry Lake Publishing, 2008.

Web Sites

FIFA

The FIFA website is a great resource to learn about the history of football around the world and how it continues to develop today.

www.fifa.com

Major League Soccer

The MLS website has up-to-date news on MLS teams, players, and standings as well as instant replays and videos of recent matches.

www.mlssoccer.com

National Women's Soccer League

For more information on women's professional soccer in the United States, you can learn about teams, players, matches, and standings on this website.

www.nwslsoccer.com

GLOSSARY

Note: Some boldfaced words are defined where they appear in the book.

adapted Changed or modified

agility The ability to move quickly and easily

association An organized group of people with a common interest

boundary lines Lines that show where the field ends

cerebral palsy A physical condition that causes difficulty in body movement

chaotic When there is no order or rules causing a lot of confusion

clubs A soccer organization that has one or more teams that compete in regional or national leagues

colonists People who leave their country and move to live in another country, bringing their rules and way of life with them

conferences In soccer, an association or league of soccer teams

disabilities Conditions that may limit one's abilities

federation A collection of organizations that work together

FIFA The international organization that makes the rules and governs soccer

hooliganism Violent behavior from people

impairments Physical weaknesses or mental conditions that make some activities challenging

marksmen People who aim at and shoot a target well

munitions Materials used for war

rebound In soccer, a rebound is when the ball bounces off something or someone and the ball is still in play

referees Officials who makes sure that the rules of the game are being followed

throw-ins In soccer, a throw-in restarts the game after the ball goes out of bounds

youth A young person

INDEX